Algunos niños tienen autismo/ Some Kids Have Autism

por/by Martha E. H. Rustad

Editor Consultor/Consulting Editor: Dra. Gail Saunders-Smith

Consultor/Consultant: Jennifer Repella, Director of Information
& Referral, Autism Society of America

CAPSTONE PRESS
a capstone imprint

Pebble Books are published by Capstone Press,
151 Good Counsel Drive, P.O. Box 669, Mankato, Minnesota 56002.
www.capstonepress.com

092009
005618CGS10

 Books published by Capstone Press are manufactured with paper
containing at least 10 percent post-consumer waste.

Library of Congress Cataloging-in-Publication Data
Rustad, Martha E. H. (Martha Elizabeth Hillman), 1975–
    [Some kids have autism. Spanish & English]
    Algunos niños tienen autismo = Some kids have autism/por
Martha E. H. Rustad.
    p. cm. — (Pebble bilingüe. Comprendiendo las diferencias = Pebble bilingual.
Understanding differences)
    Summary: "Simple text and photographs describe children with autism, their
challenges and adaptations, and their everyday activities — in both English and
Spanish" — Provided by publisher.
    Includes index.
    ISBN 978-1-4296-4593-5 (library binding.)
    1. Autism in children — Juvenile literature. I. Title. II. Title: Some kids have
autism. III. Series.
RJ506.A9R8718 2010
618.92'89 — dc22   2009030378

Note to Parents and Teachers

The Comprendiendo las diferencias/Understanding Differences set supports national
social studies standards related to individual development and identity. This book
describes children with autism and illustrates their special needs in both English
and Spanish. The photographs support early readers in understanding the text. The
repetition of words and phrases helps early readers learn new words. This book also
introduces early readers to subject-specific vocabulary words, which are defined in the
Glossary. Early readers may need assistance to read some words and to use the Table
of Contents, Glossary, Internet Sites, and Index sections of the book.

Table of Contents

Tabla de contenidos

What Is Autism?

Some kids have autism. They have trouble communicating. They might point to pictures instead of speaking.

¿Qué es el autismo?

Algunos niños tienen autismo. Ellos tienen dificultad para comunicarse. Puede ser que ellos señalen dibujos en vez de hablar.

Kids with autism might not always understand how other people feel. They might not know what a smile means.

Los niños con autismo pueden no entender cómo se sienten otras personas. Puede que ellos no sepan lo que significa una sonrisa.

Kids with autism sometimes like to be alone. Kids with autism might have trouble making friends.

Los niños con autismo a veces quieren estar solos. A los niños con autismo les puede resultar difícil hacer amigos.

Kids with autism do some actions over and over.
They might rock back and forth.
They might repeat words.

Los niños con autismo repiten algunas acciones continuamente. Ellos podrían mecerse. Ellos podrían repetir las mismas palabras.

Everyday Life

Kids with autism might have stronger senses than other kids. Bright sunlight might hurt their eyes.

La vida diaria

Los niños con autismo podrían tener sentidos más desarrollados que otros niños. La luz brillante del sol podría lastimar sus ojos.

Kids with autism go
to school. Some get
help from tutors.

Los niños con autismo
van a la escuela.
Algunos reciben
ayuda de tutores.

Kids with autism like to have the same routine every day. They like to know what will happen next.

A los niños con autismo les gusta tener la misma rutina todos los días. Les gusta saber qué pasará enseguida.

Some kids with autism
have special talents.
They might be better than
other kids at music, math,
or other skills.

Algunos niños con autismo
tienen talentos especiales. Ellos
podrían ser mejores que otros
niños en música, matemáticas
u otras habilidades.

Kids with autism sometimes like to play with their friends. Their friends can help them by being patient.

A veces a los niños con autismo les gusta jugar con sus amigos. Sus amigos pueden ayudarlos siendo pacientes.

Glossary

autism — a condition that causes people to have trouble communicating and forming relationships with people

communicate — to share information, ideas, or feelings with another person

patient — able to wait without becoming annoyed or angry

routine — a set order of actions or events

sense — one of the body's five ways of learning about the world; the five senses are taste, smell, touch, sight, and hearing.

tutor — a teacher that helps one student at a time

Internet Sites

FactHound offers a safe, fun way to find Internet sites related to this book. All of the sites on FactHound have been researched by our staff.

Here's how:

Visit *www.facthound.com*

FactHound will fetch the best sites for you!

Glosario

el autismo — una afección que causa que personas tengan problemas para comunicarse y para establecer relaciones con otras personas

comunicarse — compartir información, ideas o sentimientos con otra persona

paciente — ser capaz de esperar sin enojarse o molestarse

la rutina — una serie establecida de acciones o eventos

el sentido — una de las cinco maneras en que el cuerpo aprende acerca del mundo; los cinco sentidos son gusto, olfato, tacto, vista y oído.

el tutor — un maestro que ayuda a un estudiante por vez

Sitios de Internet

FactHound brinda una forma segura y divertida de encontrar sitios de Internet relacionados con este libro. Todos los sitios en FactHound han sido investigados por nuestro personal.

Esto es todo lo que tú necesitas hacer:

Visita *www.facthound.com*

¡FactHound buscará los mejores sitios para ti!

Index

Índice

Editorial Credits

Strictly Spanish, translation services; Katy Kudela, bilingual editor; Kim Brown, designer; Eric Manske, production specialist

Photo Credits

All photos by Capstone Press/Karon Dubke, except cover by EyeWire (Photodisc)